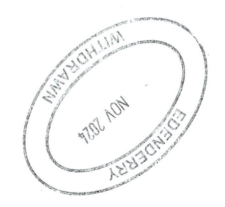

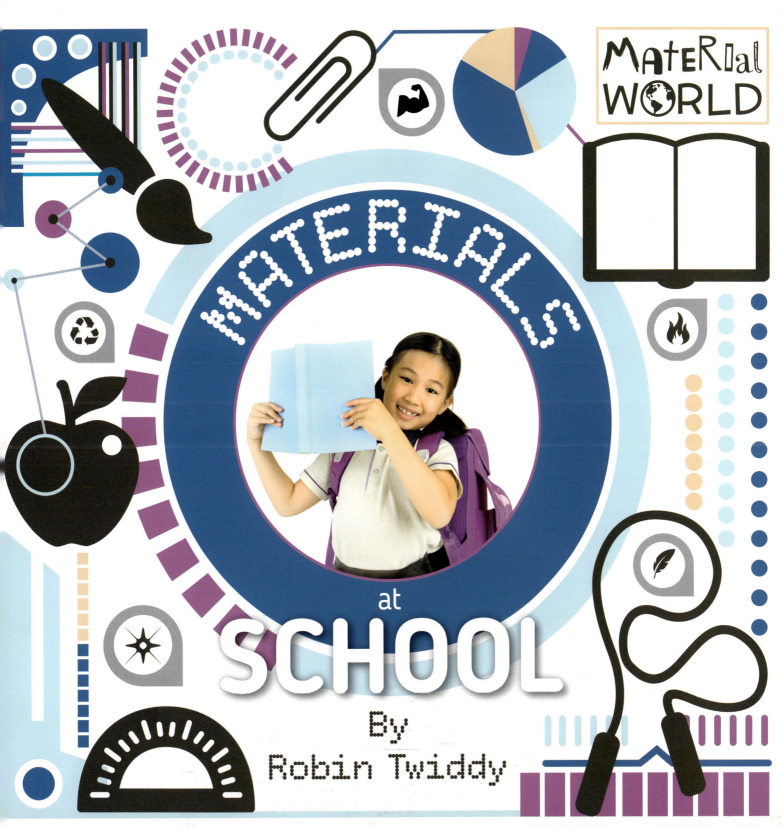

MATERIAL WORLD

MATERIALS
at
SCHOOL

By
Robin Twiddy

BookLife
PUBLISHING

©2019
BookLife Publishing
King's Lynn
Norfolk PE30 4LS
All rights reserved.
Printed in Malaysia.

A catalogue record for this book
is available from the British Library.

ISBN: 978-1-78637-445-5

Written by:
Robin Twiddy

Edited by:
Kirsty Holmes

Designed by:
Danielle Jones

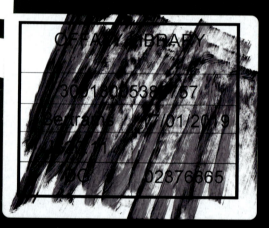

IMAGE CREDITS

Cover – wong sze yuen. 4 – Africa Studio. 5 – focal point.
6 – ESB Professional. 7 – Anna Krasovskaya, donatas1205.
8 – DGLimages. 9 – MoonBloom, Michael R Ross.
10 – AndrewHeffernan. 11 – Color Symphony, 3d_kot.
12 – NadyaEugene. 13 – Thawornnurak. 14 – Monkey Business
Images. 15 – 4otogen. 16 – haireena. 17 – JasminkaM.
18 – wavebreakmedia. 19 – PONGPIPAT.SRI. 20 – KK Tan.
21 – BestPix, Evgeniya Anikienko. 22 – RSTPIERR.
23 – hidesy, pryzmat, Brian A Jackson. Images are courtesy
of Shutterstock.com. With thanks to Getty Images, Thinkstock
Photo and iStockphoto.

CONTENTS

PAGE 4   WE'RE LIVING IN A MATERIAL WORLD

PAGE 6   A MATERIAL DESK

PAGE 8   FLOORS

PAGE 10   CLOAKROOM

PAGE 12   PLAYGROUND

PAGE 14   UNIFORMS

PAGE 16   PAINTING

PAGE 18   BOOKSHELVES

PAGE 20   CHALKBOARD

PAGE 22   MATERIAL MAGIC

PAGE 23   IN YOUR SCHOOL

PAGE 24   GLOSSARY AND INDEX

Words that look like <u>this</u> can be found in the glossary on page 24.

WE'RE LIVING
IN A MATERIAL WORLD

Have you ever thought about what things are made of? Everything in your school is made of something: wood, paper, plastic, glass... These things are called materials.

Schools, and everything in them, are built and made using materials.

All materials have <u>properties</u>. We can describe a material using its properties, such as how hard or soft it is.

Let's have a look at the materials in your school.

This exercise book is made of paper, card and glue.

Dull

Smooth

Flexible

A MATERIAL DESK

Think about your desk. What materials do you think it is made from? A lot of school desks are made from wood, with metal legs.

Some school desks are made from plastic.

Desk

Wood can be rough or smooth, dark coloured or light coloured. <u>Sanding</u> wood will change it from rough to smooth. Would you want a rough desk or a smooth desk?

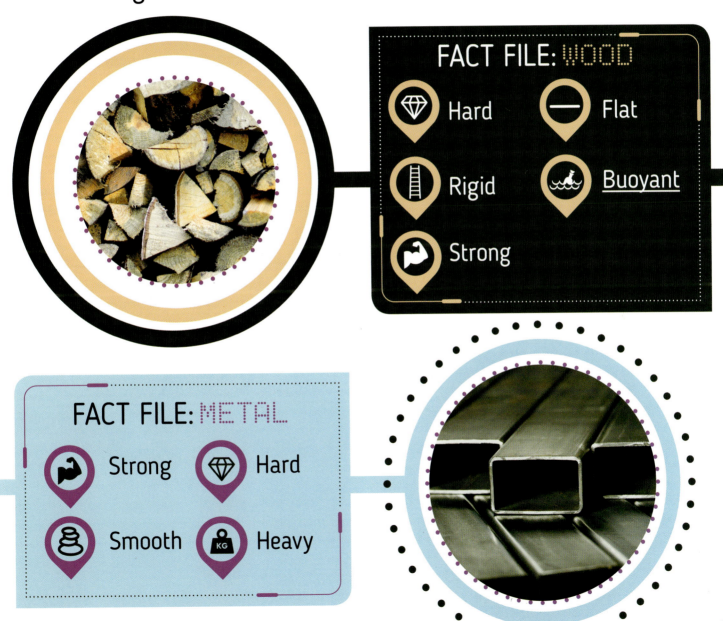

FACT FILE: WOOD

◆ Hard   ▬ Flat

▦ Rigid   〜 <u>Buoyant</u>

💪 Strong

FACT FILE: METAL

💪 Strong   ◆ Hard

⬢ Smooth   KG Heavy

FLOORS

What is the floor like in your classroom?

This classroom has carpet on the floor.
Perfect for story-time!

Carpets can be made from lots of different materials. This carpet is made from <u>nylon</u> and wool. The two materials are <u>woven</u> together to make the carpet.

FACT FILE: WOOL

 Soft

 <u>Absorbent</u>

 Strong

 Natural

 Flexible

FACT FILE: NYLON

 Strong

 Waterproof

 Smooth

 Man-made

 Flexible

CLOAKROOM

Do you have a special room to hang your coat and bag? What are the hooks made of? These hooks are made of steel and painted brightly.

Materials are often painted or dyed to make them look nicer. These hooks are painted with an enamel paint. It is a <u>liquid</u> that dries very hard.

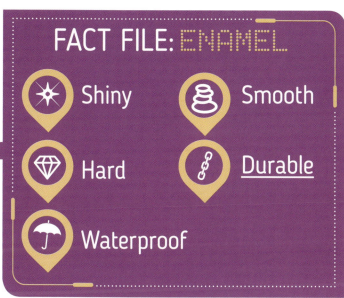

FACT FILE: ENAMEL

- ✴ Shiny
- 💎 Hard
- ☂ Waterproof
- ⬗ Smooth
- 🔗 <u>Durable</u>

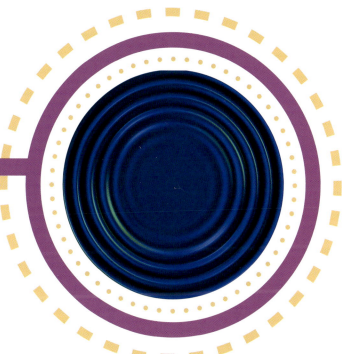

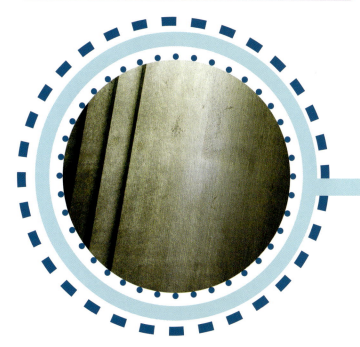

FACT FILE: STEEL

- 💎 Hard
- ⬗ Smooth
- ⤯ Flexible
- ✴ Shiny

PLAYGROUND

What is the ground in your playground made of?

Tarmac

This playground has tarmac for the children to play on.

Tarmac, also known as asphalt, is a good surface for playgrounds. Its rough surface means that shoes can grip really well.

FACT FILE: TARMAC

- 💎 Hard
- 🚫 Dull
- 📏 Rough

Tarmac is really tough so it does not wear out easily.

UNIFORMS

Do you have a school uniform? These uniforms are made from different fabrics. Fabric is made from woven <u>fibres</u>.

Fabrics can be thick or thin.

There are lots of different fabrics. This uniform is made from wool and cotton.

FACT FILE:
COTTON

Strong

Soft

Thin

Flexible

Light

PAINTING

Paint is an art material. This means that it is used to make art. But what do you think this paintbrush is made of?

16

This paintbrush is made from three materials: wood for the handle, hair for the bristles and metal for the ferrule.

Bristles can be made from animal hair or plastic.

Wood

Metal

FACT FILE: PLASTIC

Flexible

Absorbent (when bunched together)

BOOKSHELVES

Many books are made from card, paper and glue. The words and pictures are printed on the paper with ink.

Have you ever noticed that some paper is shiny? That paper is covered with a very thin layer of plastic. This makes it tougher.

FACT FILE: PAPER
- Soft
- Flexible
- Rough or Smooth

The door is made of wood and glass. There are lots of different types of wood.

FACT FILE: GLASS
- Hard
- Smooth
- Transparent

FACT FILE: WOOD
- Hard
- Smooth
- Strong
- Floats in Water

CHALKBOARD

Some schools have chalkboards; does yours? These are special boards that you can write and draw on using chalk. They are easy to wipe clean.

Sticks of chalk are used to write on chalkboards.

This chalkboard is made of wood and painted in a dark paint.

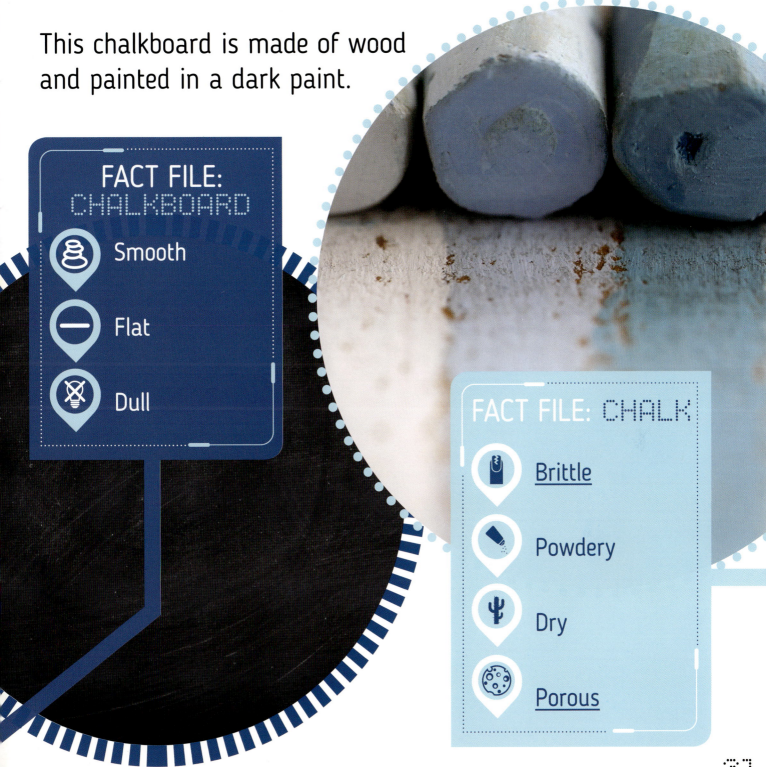

FACT FILE: CHALKBOARD

- Smooth
- Flat
- Dull

FACT FILE: CHALK

- Brittle
- Powdery
- Dry
- Porous

MATERIAL MAGIC

Did you notice that when you use chalk it makes chalk dust? The properties of the chalk change from a solid stick to a powder!

IN YOUR SCHOOL

Can you find any materials around your school that have some of the following properties:

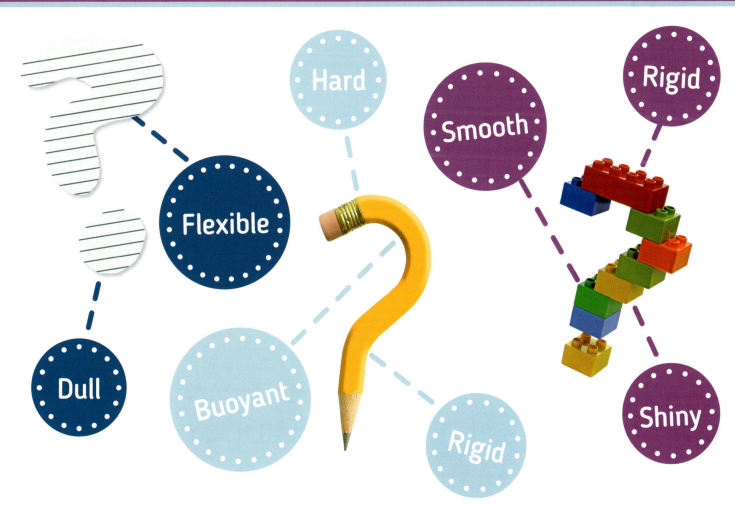

Hard

Smooth

Rigid

Flexible

Dull

Buoyant

Rigid

Shiny

GLOSSARY

absorbent	can absorb or soak up liquids
brittle	easily broken and not flexible
buoyant	can float
durable	not easily broken or worn out
ferrule	the metal part of a paintbrush that holds the bristles
fibres	things that are like threads
flexible	easily bends
liquid	a material that flows, such as water
nylon	a man-made material used to make yarn and rope
porous	having lots of small holes and being absorbent
properties	ways of describing a material
sanding	to rub with sandpaper making a material smooth
woven	made by passing threads over and under each other

INDEX

chalk 20–22

dull 5, 13, 21, 23

flexible 5, 9, 11, 15, 17, 19, 23

glass 4

heavy 7

light 15

liquid 11

man-made 9

natural 9

paint 10–11, 16–17, 21

paper 4–5, 18–19

plastic 4, 6, 17, 19

rough 7, 13, 19

sanding 7

smooth 5, 7, 9, 11, 19, 21

strong 7, 9, 15

wood 4, 6–7, 17, 21